Dharma of Death and Desire

Dharma of Death and Desire

Susannah Winters Simpson

SHANTI ARTS PUBLISHING

BRUNSWICK, MAINE

Dharma of Death and Desire

Published by Shanti Arts Publishing

Designed by Shanti Arts Designs

Cover image by Patrick Klauss and used with the artist's permission

Shanti Arts LLC
193 Hillside Road
Brunswick, Maine 04011
shantiarts.com

Printed in the United States of America

ISBN: 978-1-962082-56-3 (softcover)

Library of Congress Control Number: 2024949982

To all gentle creatures of the air, earth, and sea.

Contents

Acknowledgments

The author wishes to thank the editors of the following publications, in which poems from this collection have previously appeared or are forthcoming:

13th Moon—A Feminist Literary Magazine: "The Most Dangerous Men"

Carquinez Poetry Review: "Drive By"

Descant: "The Death of Two"

Eureka Review: "The Death of Two"

Fox Cry Review: "Trying You On"

Homestead Review: "Reprise"; "Southern Honey"; and "Tricycle"

Oregon East: "Harvest"

Pennsylvania English: "Spring at the Farm"

Quiddity: "Confessions of a Movie Junkie"; "The Oldest Profession"; and "Waterbird"

Sequestrum: "The Arithmetic of Earth, Wind, and Fire" and "History Lesson"

SWWIM: "Elegy for Kurt"

South Florida Poetry Journal: "The Eclectic Rigors of My Spiritual Practice"; "Literary Lasciviousness"; and "Word Witch"

Potomac: "Kissin' Cousins"

Weber—The Contemporary West: "Who Deserves Mercy More"

Westview: "The Eclectic Rigors of My Spiritual Practice"

Wisconsin Review: "Monday Morning Drive to Work"

The healing comes from letting there be room for all of this to happen: room for grief, for relief, for misery, for joy.

—Pema Chödrön

The Eclectic Rigors of My Spiritual Practice

Just as a redbird flashes
across my path, I long
for an epiphany.
One that erases my nagging
suspicion of chaos as supreme.
I'd like a favor from faith,
fiery baptism into an explanation,
an eureka! Even I can laugh at a joke
well told. Feverish, I search for a code
to follow, carved tablets to honor,
liturgy to memorize, even argue with,
or just one believable luminous being,
like the diamond solitaire of Venus
suspended off the tip of a crescent
moon—something to send a prayer
to, something like the swell of a Puccini aria
or the communion of kindness between
strangers, or stranger still, spouses.
Until then, I simply worship morning birds
in the larch and the didactic loyalty of our dogs.

But on an ordinary evening, a book
falls off the shelf, bookmark in place;

     I rush over to see what sign is sent.

Word Witch

On August nights the words:
summer and *heat*
evaporate from her sweat while
above her head the words:
grotto and *gallinule*
form a wreath as she sleeps
and *aphrodisiac* and *Isle of Langerhans*
move over to make room in her bed.
She pays the woodman with words
like: *thank you* and *it's perfect*
to build more shelves for fat volumes
of words in Italian and French,
for dictionaries—revised, unabridged,
and annotated and for biographies,
fables, and fiction. Her lovers
are synonyms and eponyms
and her walks on the beach
leave the imprint:
             foot   *foot*
         foot
in the sand.
She spoons sonnets out of her soup
and letters form from her tossed
apple skins.
Tomatoes in the garden
climb up in red words:
Hardy Boy and *Heirloom* and
the columbine, the lupine know
to speak to her and say: *purple* or
yellow blossom,   here   and   here   on my stalk.
The river whispers: *water* and *ripple*
and the wind, too, knows to say: *gust* or *blow.*

In April, the calamondin tree is hung
with the words:
   orange globe
       tart fruit
     bird treat
and in May the frangipani understands her need to read:
     fragrant flower
lettered along its branches.

Communion

Cousin Tom dragged two kayaks
down the rocky shore of Puget Sound,
and pushed us off onto the cold
black water. It was early morning.
The birds and homes surrounding
the inlet still sleeping,
only the rhythm of our paddles
could be heard. Just ahead, just under
the surface of the water, millions of clear
jellyfish formed a clear, cobbled route
that reached across the inlet.
For a moment: no boat, no paddles,
no legs folded in the boat, no arms reaching,
only the crisp air, the cold black water, the jellyfish.

An Unrepentant Life

I suppose I could've been on a bowling team, owned a
purple bowling jacket with *Mitzi* embroidered in white,
or sung "Sweet Caroline" along with the Cheektowaga
crowd in the beer tent at Octoberfest. Maybe I should've
been a 4-H mother, entered blue-ribbon pies or calves
into the county fair, or should've collected antique quilts,
joined the Junior League or perfected my tan, my bridge or
golf game. And, I guess especially I should have promised
to honor and obey. But instead, I struggle to stay married,
struggle to be civil, recall my tangos with Frankie, read
romance novels late into the night, and I watch B movies,
where characters with names like *Bud* call women: *dame*
or *doll*, and speak out of the corner of their mouths, saying
things like: *I ain't gonna do it, see?*

History Lesson

Overnight,
miniature mushrooms
appear in a circle on the lawn
and in the garden, Oriental lilies
open, then hang their heavy heads
and it seems, just as suddenly,
this boy leaves for his life,
where he will fail a few classes,
kiss a few women, but will
never again need milk money
or a school trip permission slip
signed, and will never again need
tagboard at ten Sunday night
for a project on Ancient Greeks:
due Monday.

Tricycle

There is a picture of us, I am 2½ and you,
with your hair already thinning, are bent over
my tricycle. We are oiling the pedals and are
bent over the same way: hands on knees as we
watch the pedals spin. It was always the same
with us, me standing close enough to hand you
a tool. While you were woodworking,
I stood nearby, but my brother read *MAD* magazine
or listened to his albums. He never asked what
to shim meant or how to string a plumb line.
So, when I bought my first home, paying $100.00
a month for #63 in Trailerama, you called
from across the country and asked me what I wanted
for Christmas: an electric drill with a sanding attachment.
You sent the money, I chose it, wrapped it, put it under the
tree and waited to open it until Christmas morning.
Now, my stepsons lose my ball-peen hammer, break off
the tip of my flathead in the wheels of their skateboard,
and leave the can of WD-40 to rust in the driveway.
Since my brother's sons will inherit your tools
and the antique miter box, I wish for a daughter
who loves the smell of sawdust, admires the golden curl
of wood shavings, and can drive a nail into an oak plank
with three strokes.

I Wanted to Be Catholic,
So I Became a Theater Major

Buffalo, New York, 1966

As a child, I had to go to Sunday School,
but there was very little talk of sin,
venial, mortal, or otherwise.
Mortification of the flesh was never
even *mentioned* in our household.
There weren't any rules about things
like no meat on Wednesday or Fish Fry Friday,
or giving up, say, ice cream
in the weeks before Easter,
or telling someone in a darkened booth
all your secrets *before* you ate the body
of Jesus and drank his blood.
I didn't know what Maundy meant
or why it was put in front of Thursday,
but I liked the way it sounded
and I learned to say the Hail Mary
the way one would memorize
words to a favorite song.
In church, my Catholic friends
wore lace circlets on their heads
and around their necks, thin silver
chains hung with tiny medals,
enameled faces of saints on them.
Everything in the Presbyterian church
was painted semigloss eggshell white,
but the insides of their churches
were so fancy and dramatic,
marble founts with Holy Water,

velvet kneelers, jeweled rosaries,
and Latin mass! So much pageantry!
Altar boys in a crisp white processional,
smoking censer swinging incense,
here and there. The priests' costumes,
matching the season's deep purple
or green satin altar cloths trimmed in gold,
so many elaborate, embroidered ways.
For Easter and the Feast of St. Joseph,
the church ladies baked sacred breads,
gilded eggs embedded in braided
golden loaves. And every church
had their own full-sized, realistically
crucified statue of Jesus, head tilted
to one side in agonized repose with a prickly
Crown-of-Thorns and shiny droplets
of blood on his brow.
Always nearby, the Blessed Mother,
Mary, Queen of the Sea
looked on with terrible sadness.
But I knew, even then, her bare foot
on the curled Serpent of Sin,
burning torch in her Sacred Heart,
she offered mercy to all.

Who Deserves Mercy More?

Who deserves to have mercy
more than I do?
Haven't I the full measure
of awfulness, human
mistakes, loss, lust?
If I could hold mercy
in my heart, keep my
heart merciful for all
that has pierced it
and bloodied it, all
that squashes and frightens
me, if I could hold
in my hand the bird
of me, coax the smallest
of me from beneath
beach shells, who more
than I needs this kindness?
Who more than I
needs to be bathed
one limb at a time,
to have the sweat
and snot and stink washed away,
soothed, kissed away,
then tucked and cradled
        into a downy sleep?

Cloistered Sister

I watch the sky darken
outside your window,
listening (as I have for months)
to your familiar talk

about insulin, your aching feet,
and that lazy Sister Magdalena.
Then, just as the sun
passes behind a cloud,

I hear you stepping out over
the narrowest of Catholic footbridges:
I'm afraid.
I don't know what is next.

And if you don't, Sister, who the Hell does?
I'm afraid I will die alone
or worse. In a nursing home like Sister Agnes,
who went to bed after dinner,

and when they came to bathe her
early the next morning,
they found her hands up
stiff in an outstretched plea.

The Brothers of Mercy Nursing Home

Each night from 7:00 to
3:00—
   pounding her fist
     against thin walls,
       oblivious to Sweeny
in 122 B,

she pleads

         accuses

and tries

   to make sense

out of

being

            left behind.

Raging

   back and forth

     to and from

locked exits

         she cries,

You couldn't have meant
                    to leave me
                              here.

Not here,
you couldn't have meant
                    to leave me
                              here.

Not here!

You couldn't mean

                    to leave me here.

Did you mean

to leave??

              And me
                    here?

Missed Steps

On any given evening,
they would roll back the living room rugs,
and he would hold out his hand, saying,

Come on, Momma!
Then they would step into a foxtrot,
roll into a Lindy or slide into the swing.

He loved to tell the story
that given a chance she would
Charleston on any tabletop.

They were a well-matched pair.
He stepping left to her right,
hip length to hip,

stepping on every beat,
cha-cha promenade,
side by side,

hands catching each other
after every turn—eyes locked
knowing what came next.

ൟ

Then at a party in '84
a stroke erased her speech,
turned her right hand

into a feral claw
and imprisoned her right leg
in a flesh-colored brace.

Her Pappagallos, Etienne Aigners,
spikes, kitten heels, strappy sandals,
and spectator pumps gathered

in mourning at the back of her closet.
Still, on any given evening,

with Old Blue Eyes or Nat on the stereo,
Dad would stand, hold out his hand,
And say, "Come on, Momma!"

But stubborn and vain, she would decline,
shamed by the brace, hideous and clumping
against the dance floor.

Elegy for Kurt

Psychiatric Ward, Bed 23 Window

When pleaded with to finish
your dinner tray, you say:

I am contemplating the virtues
of the mind versus the sins of the flesh.

You believed, to feed yourself
fed all Evil in the world.

As war news blossomed on TV,
you became thinner, then cadaverous.

A doctor's son, you had been stuffed
full of promise, Catholic school and Latin verbs.

Lamb of God—you take away
the sins of the world, have mercy.

Soon your crisp, plaid shirts and khaki
pants hung and billowed, sails on the mast,

and your speech came like purple loosestrife
along the expressway, unexpected bursts of color

shuddering from the sheer force
of what passes by.

Waterbird

Pelecanus occidentalis

Fractured high above
familiar docks and pilings,
a Brown of Victorian
consequence (she of velvet
upholstery, heavy ornate frame)
was strung upon lines
and wires, then flung
down against this concrete
century.
In my arms, her power
 drained out.
I watched the papyrus
lid closing . . . closed.

Spring at the Farm

We walked—sauntered really,
brought the dogs along, passed
through the field, and paused
at the arbor vitae. The one who lingers
paused too, resting her bad leg.

There on the grass, pale
blue eggs. Five in all.
Cold. Dense. So unreal, I looked
for the pressed plastic seam,
then searched for a nest,
not one to be found.

A few paces from the tree,
one of the big, sleek rabbits.
Cold. Stretched out in the open,
stiffened on his side.

In springs passed, the dogs
have found nests of newborn
rabbits (eyes barely open)
and devoured them,
before I could stop their feral
response.

This year, the grand rabbit's
eyes are wide open.
Glass in fur. The dogs
just sniff him, and walk by.

Temple

Her brother's death,
settled in a sacred
roll under each breast,
her sister's secret
swings as a padding
of prayer on one hip;
her lover's departure
rides on the other.

The parents' passing
forms a sacrament
of twin chins;
miscarriage rubs
a mantra
between each thigh.

Temple of flesh.
Temple of sorrow.

Face of a saint,
hands of a martyr.

Slow Rolling Boil

*Swiss animal protection laws state: "The practice
of plunging live lobsters into boiling water, which is
common in restaurants, is no longer permitted."*

Captured and placed in a room-length
tank filled with seawater, aerator bubbling.
We are the main attraction
at Red Lobster chains.

Trapped relatives, jammed two and three
deep, watch and wait as diners
point through the glass.
"I'd like that big one, please."

A neighbor struggles and is lifted out,
both claws imprisoned by wide blue bands.
In the kitchen, a large stainless steel pot.
It, too, is filled with saltwater, ready, boiling.

One Less

for the Class of June 2007

Did he know then,
buried deep among us,
forty-one writers posing on a hill,
squinting into the future,
that this was final,
or that his elaborate,
exacting plan would debauch our:
Life of Letters?
His smile is broad, genuine,
open-mouthed, the same
mouth into which he would prop
his grandfather's gun.
The photograph
commemorates a shift,
completion.
We have made sweet alliances,
enemies, and overtures
we will forget.
The grass is surreal
in its green, the pond's
loosestrife high and flowery.
Summer's false assurance
stretches cool and away behind us.

Dad and Hank

Yesterday, my 87-year-old father called.
His voice breaks and quivers. He tells me
his best friend of 45 years is dead.
Hank, robust at 88, had just returned
from the beaches of Acapulco,
where he was known to wear
a red Speedo on his still lean frame.

Long before slick TV commercials
made hair replacement available to every man,
Hank had expensive hair plugs, a row of miniature
brown turnips planted across his forehead,
which I could not stop staring at as a child.
Hank was a dandy, loved expensive Italian shoes,
beautifully cut jackets, and he loved my father.
Hank teased and defended him, mollified
and defused Dad's evil temper.

After my mother's stroke,
Hank came to the hospital every day.
He would breeze in—his designer cologne preceding him
and he would sing to my paralyzed and mute mother
in her white bed: *Here she comes, Miss America!*
Hank sat at my mother's bedside, listened as my father
wept, and patted my father's shoulder as Dad wrung his
hands in despair.

After Mother's death, Hank sent my father a check
large enough to secure a place in a plush senior community,
complete with a pool, a sauna, a screening room for films,
and waiters in white cutaway linen coats.

Hank's love for my father was immutable
and today, as my father weeps on the phone,
I imagine Dad wringing his hands,
as his own death looms just beyond
the green cushion of the 18th hole.

The Arithmetic of Earth, Wind, and Fire

Those Wednesdays, we divided the sum
of our two decades on this blue planet
with our feet. "Serpentine Fire" was the rubric
as we, giddy, arm in arm, slid out and back,
laughing through drunken versions of the Hustle.
Ladies' Night—who kept count?
Glass, after glass, after glass of cheap
pink champagne and now thirty years
after our youth, four hours past
adding up the last of your equations:
inhalation, exhalation . . .
I bought a chiffon dress
of the deepest blue, in honor
of you multiplying into the cosmos.

Hospice Atrium

I step away from my desk.
Take a break. Walk toward the center of
the building, toward the sun warming
a windowed atrium. There,
a star-shaped skylight—all glass,
three stories above a sculptured
fountain where verdigris flames rise
through the water and evoke ascension,
release into the ethers. A dark blur
flashes across the pyramid of glass—
a sparrow trapped beneath
an appearance of impossible blue sky.
Below, helpless staff nurses, doctors gather,
point, and watch her futile attempt to fly up,
to escape through the architecture above her.

First Kiss, 1969

Williamsville, New York

Brand-new on the record player:
Beatles' *Sgt. Pepper's Lonely Hearts.*

Southern parents swilling bourbon
somewhere under the trees.

Paisley-shirted, older brother,
kinder than much meaner Kenny.

You had all-American
white teeth and Keds.

Now your natural grace is gone
from the pool and the tennis court,

your diplomacy missed
around the card table.

First kiss. Mikey.
In the basement, you

played lead: "Wild Thing"
on that red Christmas guitar.

First Kiss.   Mikey Anderson.
In Tenafly. A heartburst away.

On coke. Overdose. Slumped on a couch.
Spin the bottle. Kiss in the closet.

Dead.

On Duty

At night she sets the scene,

pulls up a chair,

rests her head

on her mother's

hospital bed,

places her hand

beneath the gradually

cooling one.

She constructs a tableau

of mother/daughter

devotion,

avoided,

longed for,

now manufactured

in the small,

still hours.

The Right Price

The undertaker; a little plump,
crew cut, pink-cheeked,
wore gold coins in
his French cuffs.
His van discreet gray, only
a Marine Corps emblem
on the back window: *Semper Fi.*
He made solid eye contact,
I'm sorry for your loss,
perfect timbre of sincerity.
My sister-in-law shopped
around until the price
for men to carry her mother
out of the house
was a third
of the original quote.
I'd like the flowered
bottom sheet back,

she instructed the men,
as they rolled Nanny's
now stiff and soiled body

into a zippered bag.

Handkerchief

It was peach batiste
with three French knots
tied at one corner.

The rolled hem was whipstitched
in black, an omen about the black tears
I would cry on the plane.

In first class,
men turned their faces away,
but the women asked, *Are you all right?*

Finally, in the airplane bathroom,
where every place flesh could touch
was stainless steel,

I dropped this hankie
down a louvered chute,
finished with any polite grieving.

The Oldest Profession

In the ICU, a young nurse, maybe twenty-eight, is making
her rounds. Looking into her eyes, drawn into her pupil,
you fall down a tunnel, and you see she's already dead,
twenty or thirty patients ago. But what else can she
do—all the years in nurse's training, now a mortgage and
a marriage? Instructors in crisp white lab coats failed to
mention the immense Burden of Blame. They didn't tell her
exotic machines don't save young fathers or that antibiotics
can't stop the spread or stench of infection, or that
administrators with perfect hair, spike heels, and Armani
suits would conduct off-hours inspections. They didn't
prepare her for nursing supervisors with 70 pounds of a
master's degree between them and reality, or about missed
holiday dinners, towel shortages, mixed-up medications,
and sleeping, rude or criminal orderlies. There was no talk
of mandatory overtime, or about patients treating her like
a waitress at a truck stop (where the food is too greasy or
too cold), or about families treating her like a hotel maid
responsible for finding lost dentures, glasses, hearing aids
or about doctors treating her like a hat-check girl, or worse,
like their wives, or about the inevitable bulging blue veins
that would erupt on her thighs that no amount of summer
tan can hide. No one told her about the arbitrary, absurd
dress codes: "No piercings—no tattoos."

Paradigm Shift

Death distorts your vision.
December grass holds your gaze
as if it were splendid July sugarcane.

Night hearing becomes painfully
acute as frogs roar down
at the river's edge.

Time is pulled,
a big piece of saltwater taffy
pulled out over moments

before that phone call,
between the sending
or receiving of that letter.

It covers all prior moments,
a sticky highway holding reminders
that everything can change

in a day.

Eld Inlet, Puget Sound

Fringed with old-growth forest, ochre sand bluffs
cup around a basin of black, brackish water.

The evergreens lean toward the bay.
They remember you; they nod their branches. Yes.

This was the boy who climbed down the banks,
drew fresh water from the spring,

scaled the steep sand trail back to the cabin.
A sound echoes across the bay's ink depth:

A man hammering? Is it you?
No. Eagle drops oysters onto a floating dock.

Below the waterline, galaxies of translucent jellyfish,
a pebbled path along which we scatter your grit, your sand.

A milk-white cloud, a blossom of ash and bone, hangs suspended,
hesitates, before farewell.

Preserved Sonnet

I used to hate it when you'd make jam.
All that steam, sweetened with fruit,
all that old-fashioned fuss.
Sitting around our kitchen table
forced labor in the summer heat,
pushing red currants, gooseberries,
cherries around in sieves, slick skins
and pulp, staining fingers.
Today, melancholic, almost a year
since your death, I push cans, boxed
dry goods around the pantry shelves,
my fingers find a cool, weighted jar

sealed with your rubied jam
jewel-like in my hand.

There but for the Grace of God

7:15 a.m.

When I pick her up, I smell
old gin from her breath and skin.
The whites of her eyes have
red road maps of midnight
liquor stamped into them.
Today, she has elected to erase
decades of two-fisted drinking.
She'll pay to slice off pieces
of her face, and she has sold
her carats of diamonds,
her ounces of gold in order
to purchase a fresh start.
She bartered her gems
in exchange for a surgeon
to saw and to suture, to draw
raw edges tightly up against
her cheek and jaw.

3:20 p.m.

When I pick her up from surgery,
she is pacing, smoking, and swearing.
And between critiques of my driving,
she peers into the visor's mirror—
Fabulous! she says.
Don't I look just fantastic?
The incisions are thick, blackened
worms circling both her ears.
How do I tell her that
her features are distorted,
hideous like a researcher's face
in a wind tunnel, or worse,
flattened like a child's face pressed
wistfully against the windowpane?

The Death of Two

There they were like characters
from an old-fashioned children's book.

These field mice, dormice,
complete with dainty feet and tails,
floating in clear water mirrored above
the stainless dog bowl.

I could have expected to find
a tiny umbrella or set of galoshes
tucked neatly
at the edge of the bowl.

One's eyes were open blank discs,
and the other's closed—in resignation
or realization of water, a cruel centimeter
too far down from the lip of the bowl.

Did one follow the other in mutual agreement?
Should I have looked for a very small note?
Or did a futile paw get extended—heroic
across the water ending in double loss?

Both are buried now under last year's leaves
with tender spring just starting.

Writing Session

Residential Substance Abuse Treatment Center

Framed—in an open doorway
the young man is placed at a table.
He and I stare at the weather—
I am inclined to run out
into lightning, downpour—thunder,
for a moment,
sheets of rain dissolve labels:
teacher and *student*.
He is writing to please me,
to save his life, to save my life.
Suicides are on his list;
he tells me he balances
fifty feet above,
balances on a one-inch strap.
I have a knack, he says.
A knack for balancing above
the earth, not always
wearing a harness.

Manipulation as Fine Art at
Wednesday Noon Twelve-Step Group

A Gothic show for sure.
She, the deeply wronged
young wife, betrayed.
She strokes the skin
on her baby's face,
plays with fine
tufts of hair on its head,
while she
plays to the audience,
speaks of welcoming
her own death.
If it weren't
for my children . . .
The group gasps,
palpably rising a full inch
off their seats in horror.
This ghoulish Pietà
is the Madonna
romancing Death,
as Life kicks and coos
in her lap.

My Love, Lazarus

Each year my father sends me
the same Last Will and Testament,
two weeks after her death,
Barbara's voice speaks from her cell phone
message and you, lover, asleep
after thirty-three years in memory's
rock cave, awaken,
rise from the dead,
extend your hand to me,
a shadow that flickers
on the damp cave wall, just
out of reach.

Monday Morning Drive to Work

Okay . . . I'm in a navy blazer,
wearing pearls
and a tasteful blunt bob,
total slave
to my career calendar.
Beside me a motorcycle pulls up,
a Harley,
a chopper,
full dress hog (with duals),
out of the corner of my eye
I see bare, meaty arms,
several tattoos that would
make a sailor blush, tight
black leathers and braided
hair down his back.
I want to
look more closely,
but then he might catch me
looking, and then what?
Force my car off the road?
Strip me of blazer, stockings,
modest pumps? Make me
climb on the back
wearing only pearls?
His license plate reads:

FUCK YOU

and I think,

Well . . . maybe just this once.

Drive By

I look at my classic
and realize it may need
refurbishing
before you climb into it.
Streamline the bumpers,
polish up the hubcaps,
this mid-century model
still so responsive,
waits to be stoked—
stroked
into combustion.
I shave the upholstery
on my legs
in careful anticipation
of your head beneath my hood,
priming me for another of our
                                    drive-bys.

Trying You On

Trying
you
on
like a
décolleté
black dress,
the kind
of dress that
understands its cut
and lines. It is a dress
that sets form to function
and creates longing. Trying
you on, black velvet against
my skin, steel purpose
lining. It is no dress for
an easy foxtrot or
waltz, but a dress
designed
only for
a close
mambo,
samba,
or
sweaty
tango.

Cut from Dangerous Cloth

Florida Keys, 1987

You were my first ballroom dancing,
Harley-riding, tattooed lover.
Yours weren't an old sailor's tats, blue and fading;
these were fanciful in glorious greens, turquoise,
and shades of carnelian. They covered an arm,
a leg, and your broad Irish-Italian back.
You were visiting from New York, stepped off the plane
into the Key West Airport wearing a three-piece wool suit,
black shirt, thin black tie. If clothes make the man,
you were cut from dangerous cloth.
Jack Meyer introduced us, you asked me to coffee
and I declined. You insisted. Charmed, I accepted.
Oh, the glorious seduction! Midnight at the beach,
my resistance eroding with each kiss.
We checked into the Blue Lagoon,
with its red-flocked wallpaper and walls
as thin as the sliver of soap I used in the shower.
We danced to Hall & Oates:
One on one, I want to play
that game tonight . . .
I wept into your shoulder. Surely, I believed,
distance would defeat us. But in the end,
what finished us were your Mob connections,
your bulging neck veins as you raged,
and those handcuffs hidden under the bed.

Not Polite

My desire for you is not
of a polite nature, not
of a type to stay home,
cut up meat into a stew
or baste a hem into slacks.
Instead, my desire is an
asteroid the size of Iowa,
induces tectonic shifts, is a
molten river capable of
destroying villages in its path,
is likely to reduce senators and
plebeians alike
into pillars of stone and to litter
streets hip deep in hot white ash.
My desire wears the scent of you,
as token, as branding,
while it moves forward
to plunder and take hapless
prisoners. It is the green and blue
of the ocean—it navigates
the circumference of the globe
as my tongue traces the curve
of your earlobe and it explores
jungles in the red-gold hair on your arms.
My desire for you is harlequin, jester,
the fool positioned in front of the throne,
and it is a mongrel waiting for a morsel,
waiting for table scraps to be tossed
its way.

Mango

I am mango, my man's mouth on me; lights from Chelsea's industrial complex illuminate complex lovemaking and the sighs, the smooth, the silk erupt into a cascade which we follow downstream, then float in milky green water, sheets of white beneath us, we are carried back and forth in the arms of relief and held in an uncommon understanding that this, too, is us

forces of nature
our bodies, a raft adrift
on moonlit liquid

Literary Lascivious

(Love Sonnet #57,872)

First we'd have a cup of T. S. Eliot
in a London bookshop and I would notice
your cuff links, your civilized, buffed nails
and the crisp part in your Pantene hair.
But I know it would move very swiftly,
Jonathon. It would disintegrate to me
slathering you with Shakespeare, measuring
your Dickinson against my Virginia Woolf,
then we would be discovered bucking
under a Bukowski line that will blow
your mind and I would lick Li Po off
your lower lip and want to Faulkner you,

until you are incoherent
and rambling into the night.

Loquat

This fruit you first fed me,
passion in a tart globe—

heavy brown almost obscene pit
surprising seed vesicle within

the sweet sac of flesh.

Tenderness and Audrey

You are such a *Guy* guy. You say
things like *vehicle* and *fuel*. As a chef,
you burn and cut yourself, but never
let me apply ointment, a Band-Aid or aloe. *Nah,*
you say, *I'll be fine.* Tonight, at your house,
I see a photo of you and Audrey, your ex-wife.
You are both kids on your honeymoon at Cape May.
Audrey is golden, with waist-length hair, lean limbs
folded beneath her. She is turned in to you, her eyes
meet yours, her hand on your knee. You are a feral
god—a wild mustang tamed by her touch.
Tonight, you show me around this house of echoes,
a house of Audrey's infidelities and absence. It is
a house with a rig of a sound system which can
shake the foundations, but there are no pictures
on the walls. At midnight, silence roars through
every room; its vibration wakes me from your bed.
I pad around the empty upstairs bedrooms, see
the moon from one window, the streetlamp
from another. *Come back to bed, baby,* you say.
And I do, you cup my face and touch me
until I weep, finally I fall asleep
in Audrey's husband's arms.

Southern Honey

They drive out past cowbirds in cane fields,
white puffs against coal-black soil.
They follow along a forest of electrical towers, the Iron
Giants, and pass an elaborate radio transmitter that sends signals
to Venus, the planet of love.

In the autumn—he introduces her to bees
who visit the Florida holly—tells her their honey
is pale green. He tells her melaleuca honey
is only baker's grade and that a teaspoon
of wild honey will cure her.
He tells her summer bees turn their backs to the hive,
fanning their wings to cool the queen.

He takes her to a manatee cove where silver piers
stretch into Okeechobee's water and she collects lotus
pods washed onto broken rocks. He tells her of rattlers,
of anacondas in trees, and how as a boy,
he floated past sundown,
floated out on ink-black waves.

You, Poetry

Your eyes spell out a heroic couplet
and the quatrain's measured music
is written along your limbs. Your lips
and tongue tell of wet, tercet kisses
and your chest shouts the wide
Italian sonnet's song. Inscribed
between your loins are sextets
and alexandrine alliances,

but inked upon your
Homeric heart is an ode
to my Iliad (epic victory
over vanity) and our
Odyssey of foolishness,
these decades apart.

Word Love

Delighted, you and I bathed, drenched ourselves in words,
and often, we ate crisp words at dawn with our morning coffee.

We drove through word maps: *Belle Glade, cane fields* and rested
among the green words, *tall grass, cabbage palm, soft earth.*

We watched air words soar: *hawk, vulture, kite.* Even naked
we wore flesh words: *voluptuous hip, pink nipple, small
foot.*

Now, in the dark, I rest in sleep words: *dog, sheet, blanket.*
I awaken to the three o'clock word: *You*

But cannot find its definition.

Reprise

He remembers the press of my young thigh
against his cheek, remembers the scent
of my bed and the sounds of my sighs.
He recalls the curve of my hip clad
in black satin and remembers a halo
of my hair under lamplight. He translates
the song of the dragonfly, whale, and bee
and reorders the architecture of clouds
above me. His kiss, like the razor edge
of a palm leaf, draws dark blood from my lip,
and his tongue inhabits shower droplets
as they slip between the folds of my skin.
He is the bougainvillea's purple pigment
and his absence is the surprising
prick of its thorn. His hand is the wind
rippling green water; he is North Star,
sextant, spyglass, oarlock and rudder.
In his wake, cataclysmic waves capsize,
beach, this vessel.

Kissin' Cousins

Elvis Aron and I have a standing date. Oh, yes. Once he is done with his Southern beauties, through with their pencil skirts, thick black eyeliner and spray-stiff beehive hair, he meets me, barefoot, beside the green water and as we stroll, he places his hand on the small of my back and calls me *Darlin'*. And he tells me: *It's now or never.* Of course, I always give in. After, we don't talk about books or even music—instead I take him by the hand up to the cabin and seat him at the oilcloth-covered table. I touch his soft features; I admire his slim waist and black hair, so glossy in the lamplight. I feed him fried bacon and mayo sandwiches on the white bread I am—then I help him lick the drippins off Momma's best melamine platter.

The Most Dangerous Men

The women in my family
marry the *most* dangerous men.

Oh, not dangerous
the way *you*'d think.
These are respectable men.

Men who want their wives talented,
but *not ambitious*

smart, civic-minded,
God help us, *not controversial*

well-spoken, *not outspoken*
gracious and graceful

never, never seductive.

The women in my family
marry these dangerous men,

who earn proper livings
stay on the right side of
the law—

but know the *art* and *value*
of raising an eyebrow
chaining you in an instant

to the sink.

Scoundrel Love

You couldn't help your pirate eyes
or being red-shirted irresistible.
Your salt-and-pepper boyish curls
fell forward as you ever so gently
brushed the snares, ssh-ssh ssh-ssh.
You disarmed me—called me *Satin*
Doll and *recognized the moment*
I fell in love with you. You'd spotted it,
seen it before, that oracle of female hope.
You were an injured bird,
your right elbow permanently bent
forty-five degrees into your side,
ruining life for a career drummer.
The tragic story, you see,
got you laid plenty.
You called me *Satin Doll*,
maybe meant it too,
sang it with the jukebox,
fox-trotting; me sighing, slipping
in under that broken wing of yours.

We read Hemingway, a fitting choice
since you drank and died as hard.

Naïve nursemaid, I wiped down
your blood, vomit from bathroom walls,
hired my ex-lover lawyer to defend you,
visited you and the smells of Key West
County lockup while jeering men jostled

to see my poof-sleeved dress.
In the end, it was my old black dog you missed,
how he stretched out sleeping on your stomach,
thoroughly trusting treacherous you.

Plums

Murmur a little sadly
that love fled and hid its head
—W. B. Yeats

Barefoot, hazel-eyed and bare-chested,
you picked ripe plums off that tree
and were the only man I knew who could
mop a floor, make macaroni and cheese or
pull oatmeal cookies perfect from the oven.
In your kitchen, we drank Yukon Jack,
you staring, me blushing
in the provocative silence.

Now, long married, I place my palm
on your back as you sleep.
Disappointment rises from your skin,
and the clock beside our bed ticks:
we are not
  who we were
we are not
  who we thought.

Harvest

We grew our own pumpkins
this year and they sit on the hearth,
not carved,
probably not to be eaten.
They grew out of our
compost pile, unbidden
green, curly vines
like some Jack-and-the-Beanstalk tale.
Huge, hairy leaves
reaching across the yard
and finally climbing, symbiotic
up the Norfolk pine.
There, as if we had a hybrid cross,
hung a large pumpkin
from the pine tree.

If this is what happens
when nature takes its course,
then there is hope
for a hanging harvest
inside the house too.

Surreal Reflections on a Marriage

We are the mirror posing as pond beneath the Christmas
tree and we are the toy train which follows the tracks in
only one direction. We are the city dump disguised by
new snowfall and a teenager's blemished face troweled
and sealed over into perfection. We are a dream of Miami
moonlight, of jacarandas at the window, parrots in trees
and lavender- scented sheets all damp and mildewed with
sea spray. Our coupling is a clubfooted cancan dancer
jammed into slingback shoes who desperately hikes her
skirt higher while she missteps to crazy accordion tunes
and finally we are that ordinary room painted high gloss
Magenta Twilight, furnished in Kmart lawn chairs and lit by
flickering electric candles.

Come Hither—Cantaloupe

What a surprise,
Cantaloupe—to find you
soft-fleshed and fragrant,
deep in this hard-edged
January.

Your hull hid the perfume
of you, like a woman
who places a drop of scent
only at her collarbone,
inviting lovers to come
closer, closer.

Holistics and naturopaths
warn—eat only seasonal fruit,
but what grows and fruits
in this frozen climate?
Our winter larder
holds only wizened
fruit.

You, Cantaloupe—
remind me of exotic destinations,
of water-like air, and another life
full of dripping, forbidden fruit.

Consumer Alert

Mothers, warn your sons,
those freshly shaved waiters,
sincere masseurs, pumped-
up pool boys—warn them
that the ferocity of my loneliness,
this knife's edge longing for you,
will peel back the nubile skin
around their hearts, will undress
and devour them, will cling
to their long, firm limbs, will grip
around their waists like a boa constrictor,
will shriek like a jungle rat into their ears,
will wreck them for any other woman,
a woman like you, who will clip
sale coupons, will shop around
for the best price on radishes,
paper towels and pork chops.

In the Last Four Days

While you were writhing on the whipping post
of your dying marriage—I used my Bushnells
to see waterbirds more clearly.
Looking skyward, I searched for the telltale
rusty patch of the red-shouldered hawk
and spotted the fabled wood stork
all white and black
and Hans Christian Andersen of him.
While you twisted, hung from mediation's
drying leather thongs, from those negotiations
which bound your wrists and ankles,
I saw an elusive brown-spotted limpkin
plucking apple snails from the shoreline.
Finally, when the last vestiges of civility
ran down your leg, the male anhinga
spread his wings for me in a double chevron,
while his mate perched and preened
her feathered bridal finery.

Mendelssohn's Song Without Words Doesn't Need Any

The cello speaks clearly:
He has finally left you for the wife,
for his children, for the dog
and the white colonial
with a beech in the backyard.

Autumn nights, he will lie in bed
facing away from his wife;
he'll watch moonlit leaves
fall from the beech tree; he will watch
it frost over, then bud in early spring.

He will fold your handkerchief
into the back of his shirt drawer
and on Sunday mornings when
the wife and children are away,
making peace with their personal
Savior, he will unfold it against
his face to see if your scent
still lingers.

Confessions of a Movie Junkie

"I think I will pack my little bags and go back to Vienna
where I belong." —Baroness Von Schraeder, *Sound of Music*

Transported to Kowloon, or Oklahoma,
I've found the Cave of Swimmers
best for grief work. As for jealousy, I prefer
artful Ben Nye, Hitchcock and Edith Head.
I find solace in gray peplum suits,
seamed stockings, opera-length gloves
and Kim Novak's improbable eyebrows.
I trust in the impossibly pointed breasts
of Shirley Jones pressed firmly against
a singing cowboy's fringed chest.

Don't include me or consult me,
forget my birthday—lust after another.
I count on sequined, celluloid resurrection.
Feathered headdresses—white muffs
and velvet skating skirts,
sure to dispel all evil.
Swimmers, swanlike in rubber caps,
kick and wave, banishing brutality in unison
while dancing men, top hats, tap shoes

pound out a rhythm of varnished truth.

Relative Loneliness

Loneliness,
the Elderly Aunt,

makes an early
Sunday visit,
and sits poised,
white-gloved,
in the parlor
long past her welcome.

In her vise-like grip,
you watch perfectly
normal clocks elongate
Dali-esque
on the mantel,
and see every particle
of dust floating
through the blinds.

Then, even
long after she leaves,
long, long after she leaves,

deep Sunday silence
can be heard
from the middle
of your bed.

Sunday and the Solar System

The Susquehanna is high,
its current swift after the rains.
I drive across the bridge and lift
my eyes to the circle of golden
hills. I watch a red-tailed hawk
swooping above the brown, unruly
river. For a moment, the air lightens
and eases the loss of your hands,
your mouth and the weight of you
upon me.
On my living room window
I stick translucent decals
of the solar system:
Saturn with its green rings,
purple Jupiter—the giant planet;
and Earth—our own blue jewel.
I wait for you and my faith
in gravity, in the seasons and tides,
renews as the sun shifts
through these plastic planets.

Film Noir

In these movies, the streets are dark
and slick with rain. The men wear
belted trench coats, have heavy five o'clock
shadows and are always spies or gumshoes.
The women have bee-stung lips and names
like Dolores, or Bette, or Agnes.
These films blot out the Friday fact
that you haven't called
and they erase the Saturday myth
that you will show up at 8:00 P.M.
with a miniature box of watercolors,
a splendid geode,
or an ancient map of the world.

Homeless

You hand me a moon shell,
rare, you think—this
yellow-pink is smooth
and warm and the exact hue
of my palm. Grains of truth,
of sand, still cling to its lip.
You offer it
with wide lagoon eyes
and a promise. You
and the mollusk are out
of your homes—as I listen,
I hear an ocean, as swells of grief
pour from its chambered
empty ear.

Dharma

It is the syntax of blue jays
and children at play—
it is the cries of a condor, or
of forbidden lovers as they soar
between twin peaks.
It is the distinct color of water
just now! No, just now,
and it is the silver mercy
of aspen leaves as they flip over.

It is the lingering fragrance
on my mother's slip, the scent
of our Sunday's rumpled sheets,
the metal taste of your blood
left on my lip. It is the popcorn smell
of the old dog's paws, the blue perfume
of a hyacinth and the surprise of yellow
beneath a cracked eggshell.

It is Mozart, "Vissi d'Arte" and the curved
shadow of our globe upon her moon;
it is calibrations of Galileo
and hues of Michelangelo.
It is Hiroshima's ash
and Buchenwald's brick,
and it is the squeeze of a widow's heart
as she hears his final breath

Peach

You opened yourself
to me—a globe of early
morning—thin clouds
of dawn surrounding
this tender meat. Juice spills
from your pink cusp onto my
bare chest—runs down
through my fingers, leaves me
sticky with liquid fragrance,
your edible perfume. Another
day, and moonrise is many hours
away from the memory
of you, a crescent of summer's
flesh, tasted and swallowed
whole.

SUSANNAH WINTERS SIMPSON is a hospice nurse. Her work has been published in *North American Review, Potomac, Wisconsin Review, South Carolina Review, POET, Nimrod International, Poet Lore, MORIA Literary Magazine, Salamander, Sequestrum,* and *SWWIM,* among others. She was chosen as a 2023 Featured Poet for Miami's SWWIM/The Betsy Hotel's Reading Series, and her poems have been included in several anthologies. Four of her poems won second prize in CommuterLit's 2023 National Poetry Contest.

Simpson was recently featured in the *Palm Beach Illustrated* April 2024 Literati section in honor of National Poetry Month. Simpson is the founder and co-director of the Performance Poets of the Palm Beaches, Imagine Women Writing Retreats, and is Founder of Palm Beach Players for Change. Simpson holds an MFA in writing and literature from Bennington College, a PhD from Binghamton University, and a Certificate of Advanced Study in therapeutic writing. She currently facilitates both creative writing and WriteRECOVERY groups.

www.ingramcontent.com/pod-product-compliance
Lightning Source LLC
Chambersburg PA
CBHW022038090426

42741CB00007B/1110